Unlocking the Secrets of Science

Profiling 20th Century Achievers in Science, Medicine, and Technology

Frederick Banting and the Discovery of Insulin

John Bankston

PO Box 619
Bear, Delaware 19701

Unlocking the Secrets of Science

Profiling 20th Century Achievers in Science, Medicine, and Technology

Frederick Banting and the Discovery of Insulin

First Printing

Library of Congress Cataloging-in-Publication Data
Bankston, John, 1974-
    Frederick Banting and the discovery of insulin/John Bankston.
      p. cm. — (Unlocking the secrets of science)
    Includes bibliographical references and index.
    Summary: Recounts the life of the Canadian doctor and how his research led to the discovery of insulin and a treatment for diabetes.
    ISBN 1-58415-094-7
    1. Banting, Frederick Grant, Sir, 1891-1941—Juvenile literature. 2. Physicians—Ontario—Biography—Juvenile literature. 3. Insulin—History—Juvenile literature. 4. Diabetes—History—Juvenile literature. [1. Banting, Frederick Grant, Sir, 1891-1941. 2. Physicians. 3. Nobel Prizes—Biography. 4. Insulin—History. 5. Diabetes—History.] I. Title. II. Series.
R464.B3 B36 2001
616.4'62'0092—dc21
[B]
                                                                 2001038019

ABOUT THE AUTHOR: Born in Boston, Massachussetts, John Bankston began publishing articles in newspapers and magazines while still a teenager. Since then, he has written over two hundred articles, and contributed chapters to books such as *Crimes of Passion*, and *Death Row 2000*, which have been sold in bookstores around the world. He currently lives in Los Angeles, California, pursuing a career in the entertainment industry. He has worked as a writer for the movie *Dot-Com*, which began filming in winter 2000, and is finishing his first young adult novel. In addition to being a writer, John is also a model and actor.

PHOTO CREDITS: cover: Archive Photos; p. 6 Archive Photos; p. 10 Photo Researchers; pp. 18, 22, 26, 38, 44, 50 Hulton Getty; p. 32 Archive Photos; p. 43 Superstock; p. 44

PUBLISHER'S NOTE: In selecting those persons to be profiled in this series, we first attempted to identify the most notable accomplishments of the 20th century in science, medicine, and technology. When we were done, we noted a serious deficiency in the inclusion of women. For the greater part of the 20th century science, medicine, and technology were male-dominated fields. In many cases, the contributions of women went unrecognized. Women have tried for years to be included in these areas, and in many cases, women worked side by side with men who took credit for their ideas and discoveries. Even as we move forward into the 21st century, we find women still sadly underrepresented. It is not an oversight, therefore, that we profiled mostly male achievers. Information simply does not exist to include a fair selection of women.

17,95

Contents

The son of a farmer, Frederick Grant Banting would grow up to discover insulin, a treatment that saved the lives of millions of diabetics.

Chapter 1

Life in the Nineties

• •

Growing up in the 1890's, Frederick Banting came of age in a time very different from our own. Someone born then often didn't live long enough to celebrate his thirty-fifth birthday. That was the average life span.

Many houses lacked running water or electricity. Although some things we use today had already been invented - such as the telephone and the electric light bulb - in rural areas, these innovations were often only read about. They weren't commonplace.

It was also a time when many diseases - from typhoid to tuberculosis - killed millions. Among the worst of these was diabetes.

In modern science, discovery of a disease often leads fairly rapidly to its cure. This was not the case with diabetes.

Four-thousand-year-old Egyptian hieroglyphics describe the illness. It was written about by Greek physicians over two thousand years ago. Arataeus described it as a "melting down of flesh and limbs."

Diabetes is a fairly complex disease. The best way to look at it, is to consider that the same way gas is fuel for our cars, food is fuel for our bodies. Someone becomes diabetic when their body can no longer utilize this fuel. The food they eat is not converted into energy, it just passes through their systems.

Diabetes is from the Greek word for "pipe-like." The digestive system of a diabetic person is turned into a "pipe," where food just travels through without being used.

When the body can no longer use the food the person eats, the victim slowly starves to death. In the 1890s, most people who got diabetes eventually went into a coma. It was almost always fatal.

The odd thing about diabetes is in many ways it's related to what could be considered a sign of success - the availability of food. When food was rare, so was diabetes. As farming practices improved and countries such as the United States, Canada, and England were better able to feed their people, diabetes became common. Even today, one of the causes of diabetes is over eating, or obesity.

By the late 1800s, millions of people worldwide were sick with the disease. In industrial countries as many as two percent of the population were diabetic.

The most common treatment was to restrict the diet of the person suffering. Food is measured in calories - most people consume around 2,000 a day. The diet for diabetics back then called for the sufferer to consume less than six hundred calories. It was a very difficult diet to stick to.

Despite the hardships of the late nineteenth century, young Frederick Banting's life was generally pleasant. Growing up on a farm in Canada, he got to work with animals and observe the cycles of life close up. Along with his cousin, Fred Hipwell, Frederick Banting enjoyed everything from exploring Scout Island on the nearby Boyne River, to helping care for the cows and pigs. However, according to some, Frederick

Banting was touched personally by diabetes while he was a teenager.

These accounts mention a young classmate. Frederick Banting saw this teenager go from being energetic to being someone who slept all the time, was groggy when awake and drank and ate ravenously. Despite the hunger, Frederick's friend continued to lose weight.

Some of the people who knew him then claimed this was one of the most important events in young Frederick's life. It was the first time he had ever heard of diabetes. When his classmate died, he asked himself why doctors - despite all their training – couldn't cure his friend.

From his friend's death to the time he spent helping the animals, Frederick Banting knew without a doubt what he wanted to do with the rest of his life. He didn't just want to help people feel better while they slowly got sicker. He wanted to cure them.

In order to become a doctor, Frederick Banting would go against his family. In order to find a treatment for diabetes, Frederick Banting would go against the beliefs of some of the most educated men of his time. Before he succeeded, he would know poverty, hunger, and would lose the woman he loved.

This is his story.

Despite the primitive conditions and crushing poverty of many of their patients, rural doctors did their best to treat a variety of illnesses.

Chapter 2

A Difficult Decision

$\mathbf{I}$n the downstairs bedroom of a white frame farmhouse in Alliston, Canada, Margaret Banting gave birth to a boy on November 14, 1891. The last of five children born to William and Margaret Banting, he was named Frederick Grant Banting, though everyone called him Fred.

Alliston is a small town in the province of Ontario, about forty miles north of Toronto. When Fred Banting was born, Toronto was Canada's second largest city with over half a million people.

Growing up in Alliston, Fred was a world away from Toronto. Alliston was like many small towns. It was the type of place where neighbors knew each other and helped each other out. As the youngest child, Fred was especially close to his mother. His father William was more of an authority figure. Usually Fred went to his mother first when he had a problem he wanted to discuss.

Attending a public school in Alliston, Fred was best known for playing hockey, soccer and baseball. In fact, he played on the Alliston High School baseball team the year they won the league championship.

Most people saw Fred as more of an athlete than a serious student. Years after he graduated, Fred's high school principal told a newspaper reporter, "We would not have picked him for one on whom fame should settle."

Despite not standing out academically, Fred Banting wanted to pursue a career in medicine. His dreams reached far beyond the rural life he knew. He was not alone.

Until the late nineteenth century, most children who were raised on farms became farmers. Fred's father was himself the son of a farmer. John Banting—Fred's grandfather—had been born in Northern Ireland and moved to Canada in the 1850s.

This was the tradition Fred Banting faced as a teenager. All around him the world was rapidly changing. Modern agricultural techniques meant that fewer and fewer people were needed to work on farms. Young adults began looking to the cities for opportunities.

The Industrial Revolution is the name given to the development of innovations which changed the lives of people born in the latter part of the 1800s. From electric light bulbs to internal combustion engines, a wave of discoveries changed the way people lived.

These discoveries were not limited to the world of machines. In medicine, for example, improved microscopes changed the ways scientists studied cells. By examining cell samples, scientists like France's Louis Pasteur and Russia's Elie Metchnikoff learned new ways to combat disease.

Fred Banting wanted to be a part of all that. He didn't want to be like the country doctors he knew, men who could offer little more than kind words while their patients died. Banting wanted to become a doctor in a new era, the twentieth century, where doctors were learning how to cure patients, not just comfort them. Unfortunately, while Fred Banting wanted to be a doctor, his father had other ideas.

William Banting was a trustee in the Methodist church. He believed that the most important thing one of his sons could do was become a minister. Since his older boys Nelson, Thompson, and Kenneth had already pursued other ambitions, William's last hope for a son in the ministry fell on Frederick. As a teenager, therefore, Fred quickly realized that the greatest obstacle he faced was in his own household.

Fred Banting respected his father. The last thing he wanted to do was disappoint him. Yet in his heart, Fred Banting knew he wanted to be a doctor.

His cousin, Fred Hipwell, faced a similar challenge. Like Banting, Hipwell wanted to be a doctor. Like Banting, Hipwell had parents who wanted him to pursue the ministry. The two discussed their dilemma. Eventually they found a solution. They would become medical missionaries!

By combining their dreams with those of their parents', the pair would be able to pursue medicine and religion. In the beginning it seemed like a flawless plan.

William Banting was pleased by his son's choice, but Frederick's mother Margaret was concerned. She knew the life of a missionary overseas was very dangerous. Many died from fatal illnesses like malaria, and some were killed by natives of the countries where they worked. Despite these worries, in the end the cousins' parents agreed.

In the fall of 1910, Frederick Banting and Fredrick Hipwell registered at Victoria College in Toronto. The two would study religion and then later on would study medicine. They also roomed together, in a boarding house near the school.

College life was not easy for Banting. Although tall by the standards of the time—he stood more than six feet—and athletic, he was also very shy. He had difficulty meeting women or socializing. He also had a hard time concentrating on his studies. His grades were terrible; he began to fail in some of his classes.

Like many young people, Frederick found himself torn between pleasing his parents and following his dreams. He didn't want to wait to become a doctor. He wanted to begin studying medicine immediately.

During the Easter break of his sophomore year, Banting went home to Alliston. By then he'd realized that studying religion was a mistake. He didn't want to be a missionary. He wanted more than ever to be a doctor.

Fred Banting discussed his dilemma with the town's Methodist minister. The minister convinced Banting to tell his parents. Nervously, Banting did— that very night. Instead of criticizing him, his parents supported his decision. Banting realized he'd gotten himself worked up over nothing. His father was still proud of him.

In the fall of 1912, Fred Banting enrolled in medicine at the University of Toronto. The medical school had one of the highest student enrollments in North America and was very well equipped. Its teaching hospital—Toronto General—had recently been rebuilt and was considered one of the best in the world.

Both the hospital and the university were becoming increasingly focused on the research part of medicine. Fred Banting knew how important medical research would be in finding cures for many of the diseases that plagued people in the early part of the twentieth century. Diseases such as typhoid fever, tuberculosis—and diabetes.

As part of the "Meds Seventeen" class, Banting was joined by his cousin Fred Hipwell. Hipwell had followed his cousin's lead and told his own parents about his ambitions. Both young men looked forward to a five-year course of study within the large white brick building which housed the medical school.

Fred Banting's love life was improving too. Edith Roach, the daughter of the Methodist minister he'd confided in, was a languages student nearby. The pair began dating.

He was finally following his dream. Still, Banting's grades were only average. But even though he wasn't a star academically, Banting had a focus and determination beyond his fellow students. While others relied upon lab technicians to prepare the tissue samples they studied, Banting prepared his own. He was also one of the few students to purchase his own microscope. It cost fifty-seven dollars, a lot of money in the early 1900s, but to Banting it was worth it.

Banting regularly would prick his finger and study the blood beneath the microscope. By doing this he became very adept in hematology, the study of blood. His knowledge of hematology quickly surpassed that of his fellow students.

Banting would later recall one lecture over all the others. A professor of biochemistry named A.B. McCallum spoke about the oblong shaped gland in the digestive system known as the pancreas. Within the pancreas are groups of cells known as the "islands of Langerhans," named after their discoverer, Paul Langerhans.

Like Banting, Langerhans was a curious medical student in Germany who spent a great deal of time looking through the lens of his microscope. In 1869, he was looking at a piece of pancreas and saw tiny bunches of spots, which looked like islands to him. They were unlike regular pancreas cells because they did not lead to the intestines—they were "ductless."

McCallum presented a mystery to his class: what were those cells for? The islands of Langerhans produced something scientists called Hormone X. It was absorbed by the body in a way they did not understand, but somehow it prevented diabetes.

Unfortunately, no one knew how to obtain this substance.

McCallum called Hormone X the "secret treasure" on the islands of Langerhans. "Perhaps someday, someone in this class will be the one to find this secret treasure," McCallum said.

Although the lecture stayed with him, there were many other areas of medicine Fred Banting had to learn. He was particularly interested in orthopedic surgery, and considered the repair of injuries and correction of deformities to be a possible focus for his career.

But Frederick Banting's life as a medical student was abruptly changed by events thousands of miles away.

In the early summer of 1914, Archduke Franz Ferdinand, the heir to the throne of the vast empire called Austria-Hungary, was assassinated in Serbia. Before long all the countries of Europe, along with the United States and Canada, were dragged into the conflict which eventually became known as World War I, or as it was called at the time, the Great War.

The war would shorten Frederick Banting's medical studies.

It would also come close to ending his medical career forever.

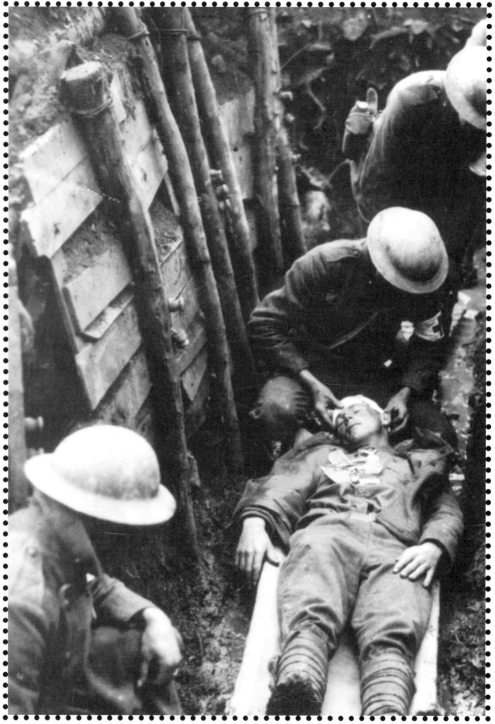

The horrors of trench combat during World War I provided an opportunity for battlefield surgeons like Banting to hone their skills.

Chapter 3
The Great War

● ●

By 1915, Fred Banting had joined the Canadian Officers Training Corps. His studies at the university now included time for marching and military preparation.

His medical class, which had been scheduled to graduate in 1917, finished a year early because of the drastic need for medical professionals overseas. The class took its fifth year over the summer of 1916. "I had five pages of notes on the whole lectures of the fifth year," Banting recalled in his memoirs, and "a very deficient medical training." Those deficiencies would not last long.

Regardless of whether a particular war can be considered just or not, all wars are horrific in the lives they cost. Wars kill thousands, sometimes millions, of people. But despite the horrors of combat, there is at least one benefit. Doctors' skills are greatly improved. A wartime surgeon can see more patients in a year or two than a civilian surgeon might see in a lifetime. Doctors learn quickly how to treat a variety of injuries and how to combat infectious diseases.

After Banting passed his tests and graduated from the University of Toronto, he asked Edith to marry him. She said yes. But before they could be married, Banting was shipped out to Granville Canadian Special Hospital in Buxton, England.

His job involved setting the wounds and repairing the shattered bones of injured soldiers. They came in from the "front lines" in France, where the actual fighting was taking place. At his location, Banting was safely far away from combat. He hated this.

He felt strongly that safe posts like the one at Buxton should be reserved for older doctors, men with wives and children. As a young surgeon, Banting believed he shouldn't be in England. He should be in France, close to where the men were being wounded.

After over a year in Buxton, he received the assignment he wanted. He was transferred to the Thirteenth Field Ambulance Corps and sent to the front lines in France.

Banting developed a reputation among his fellow doctors and his superior officers for how sensitive he was with the wounded soldiers. While many other doctors wouldn't hesitate to cut off an injured limb, Banting would do everything he could to save it. All he could think about was what life would be like for a wounded man who returned home with a missing arm or leg.

So Banting worked extra hard, in hopes that the soldiers he treated would not face amputation. This focus on others would eventually touch his own life.

In the autumn of 1918, the Allies—the United States, England, France and Canada—were poised to launch an attack against the Germans that might finally end the war.

In September, the second battle of Cambrai began. On the 28th, Captain Banting was busy treating the injured in a bombed-out barn. Artillery exploded. A piece of shrapnel—a razor-sharp piece of steel from an exploding shell—lodged in Banting's arm. His forearm almost split in two, and an important artery was partially severed.

His superior officer, Major L.C. Palmer, commanded Banting to get into an ambulance. But when Major Palmer was called away moments later, Banting realized there were no other surgeons available to treat the injured. If he left, solders would die. So Banting applied a tourniquet—a tight bandage—to his injured arm and kept working. Seventeen hours later, Major Palmer returned. Banting was still conducting first aid. This time the major made sure Captain Banting got into the ambulance. Banting would receive the Military Cross—one of Canada's highest honors—for courage under fire at Cambrai.

But receiving a decoration was not the most important thing on Banting's mind as he returned to his old hospital in Buxton, England. This time he was a patient. The doctors had bad news. They wanted to amputate.

Captain Banting realized how his life would change. If they cut off his arm, he wouldn't be able to be a surgeon. His dreams would disappear. He thought of the doctors he'd seen in combat, who sometimes didn't consider options other than amputation. So Banting stubbornly refused the advice of all the other doctors. He suffered through a long healing process, and by carefully caring for his injury, saved his arm.

It was time to go home.

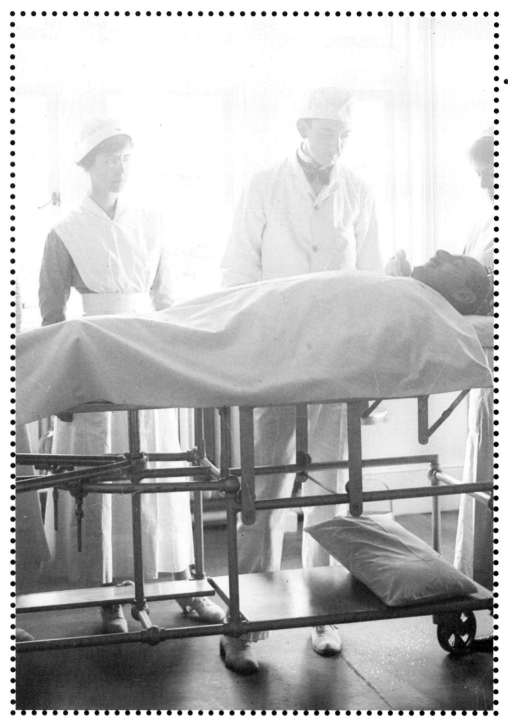

Although primitive by modern standards, hospitals in the early twentieth century were already developing many of the surgical techniques used today.

Chapter 4

Late Night Reading

World War I was over. Having spent a year in England recovering from his injuries, Captain Banting was ready to become Doctor Banting and go back to Canada.

Dr. Clarence L. Starr, a mentor to the young doctor, was Chief Surgeon at the Hospital for Sick Children in Toronto. He offered Banting a job as a surgical resident. This meant Banting would be able to continue his training in surgery, but he would not actually have a staff job with the hospital.

Banting saw the position as an opportunity to work under one of the top surgeons in Canada. He began working at the hospital in September of 1919. Doctors were just beginning to specialize in particular areas of medicine. At that time, Banting knew he wanted to specialize in orthopedics. He began to focus on treating children with crooked backs, club feet and missing limbs.

Banting was still very shy with adults. However, with his young patients Dr. Banting shared a special bond. The other doctors were impressed by how easily Banting related to the children.

Many of the children he saw were also very shy, a result of their disfigurements. Although Dr. Banting hid his war wound from adults, he gained the children's trust by revealing the lengthy scar on his arm. It was his way of letting them know that it was possible to overcome disability.

But despite Banting's hard work and popularity, he found it impossible to advance beyond surgical resident. "Surgeons were very plentiful in Toronto," he recalled in his memoirs. "It was my greatest ambition to obtain a place on the staff of the hospital, but this was not forthcoming."

Dr. Starr, along with some of Banting's friends, advised the young doctor that Toronto wasn't the best place for him. In Toronto the doctors were older and more established. London, Ontario offered more opportunities for younger doctors.

Over one hundred miles from Toronto, London was the second largest city in Western Ontario. In London, the University of Western Ontario's medical school was in the process of being rebuilt. When completed, it would boast some of the finest facilities for medical research available. While he'd loved his work at the hospital, Banting had missed doing research.

As added incentive, his fiancee Edith Roach planned to teach at a high school near London. Although he wanted to get married, he refused to do so until his career became more stable. Moving could be the chance of a lifetime. Unfortunately, the twenty-eight-year-old was flat broke. So Banting did what many young people do when they need money. He asked his parents.

William Banting loaned his son several thousand dollars. Dr. Banting used it to make the down payment on a white brick house at 442 Adelaide Street North in London. The former home of a shoemaker, it would serve as both office and residence for Banting. Along with some borrowed family furniture, he moved in on July 1, 1920. He hung up his sign and waited for business. He did a lot of waiting.

Dr. Banting didn't see his first patient until July 29, and the man he saw wasn't even sick. He just wanted liquor, hoping to get around the province's prohibition laws which made alcohol illegal.

By the end of July, Banting had earned a grand total of four dollars. He cut back on expenses, and even used his Bunsen burner to cook meals. Things looked bleak.

In October, Banting was offered a job at the University of Western Ontario. As a part-time demonstrator and lecturer, he earned two dollars an hour. Despite the hardships, there was one advantage to the lack of business in Banting's private practice. He had a great deal of free time. He studied the latest medical journals, becoming such a regular at the university library that the librarians set aside the newest issues for the doctor.

When the November issue of "Surgery, Gynecology, and Obstetrics" came out, the timing was perfect. Banting had been thinking about a lecture he was scheduled to give on the pancreas, the organ about which biochemistry professor McCallum had spoken several years earlier. In the magazine, Banting found an article on how the islands of Langerhans in the pancreas related to diabetes.

Between the article and the next day's lecture, Banting spent a restless night. Because he couldn't fall asleep that night, Banting would eventually make a discovery that finally freed him from all his problems.

Small in stature but huge in influence, Dr. J.J.R. Macleod gave Banting his first chance to test his theories concerning the mysterious Hormone X.

Chapter 5

2:00 A.M. Discovery

● ●

On October 31, 1920, unable to sleep, Dr. Fred Banting got out of bed and opened his notebook. He jotted down these words: "Ligate pancreatic ducts of dogs. Wait six to eight weeks for degeneration. Remove the residue and extract."

Those words would lead to a discovery which would change the lives of millions of diabetics.

What Banting realized that night is how a functioning pancreas—whether in a dog or a person—might prevent doctors from successfully extracting the Hormone X produced by the islands of Langerhans cells. Those cells, which exist within the pancreas alongside normal pancreatic cells, were destroyed by digestive fluid whenever they were removed from the pancreas. By ligating, or tying off, the ducts of the pancreas, Banting guessed he could cause the pancreas itself to atrophy, or wither, during a period of six to eight weeks. The pancreatic cells that generated digestive fluids would die during that time.

But the islands of Langerhans cells should still be healthy and could then be safely removed as a residue because the digestive fluids that otherwise would have destroyed them would be gone. He could remove the residue, those still healthy cells. He felt he could then inject the residue into a diabetic dog and cure it. Since dogs had similar organs to human beings, what worked on dogs should also work on humans.

Banting's breakthrough left him so excited he had a hard time sleeping. Throughout his lecture the next day, he kept thinking about his discovery. He wanted to test it, do the research he'd described in his notebook. But first he had to convince others. That wasn't easy.

He visited Dr. F.R. Miller, the chief of the physiology department at Western University. Dr. Miller had done some very promising tests involving the brain. However, when Banting approached him, Dr. Miller said that he was too involved with his own work. Besides, Western didn't have the proper facilities to conduct experiments on dogs. For that, Banting would have to go back to Toronto.

Banting couldn't believe it. He'd only left the city a few months before, and now everyone he spoke with told him the same thing. If he wanted to conduct his experiment, he'd have to give up his life in London. Banting decided the risk was worth it.

Coincidentally, Banting already had plans in Toronto the next weekend. The daughter of Dr. Starr, his old mentor, was getting married.

At the wedding reception, he couldn't stop talking about the idea. "I wished to give up practice in London immediately and commence work," he recalled in his 1940 memoirs. His friends thought it was a crazy idea, and all of them advised him not to do it. Banting wouldn't give up.

On Monday, November 7th—just a week after he'd had the idea—Banting sat down in the office of one of the most prestigious faculty members at the Toronto Medical School. Dr. J.J.R. Macleod was the man everyone told him to see. Although small in stature, he was huge in influence. He was considered one of the leading authorities on sugar chemistry. It would be his decision whether or not the university would help Banting.

Dr. Macleod didn't believe that Hormone X existed in the islands of Langerhans. In other words, Banting was trying to get assistance from someone who already didn't agree with him.

Worse, Banting was a surgeon, rather than a medical researcher, and he wasn't very well known. The only reason Dr. Macleod even met with him was because Banting had graduated from the medical school.

"I found that Dr. Banting had only a superficial textbook knowledge of the work that had been done on the effects of pancreatic extracts in diabetes," Macleod would later write of their first meeting. "He had very little practical familiarity with the methods by which such a problem could be investigated in the laboratory."

Banting could tell the meeting didn't go well. He later wrote in his memoirs that "apparently my subject was not well presented, for he commenced to read the letters on his desk."

Having been rudely ignored, most people would have given up. But Banting had two things going for him: his passion for the experiment, and the fact that no one had tried it before.

The next day, Banting called Macleod first thing in the morning. He begged for another meeting. Banting got his wish. When he went to Macleod's office that afternoon, he was surprised by the professor's change in attitude. Dr. Macleod suddenly seemed interested in the idea, and had even done some research.

He told the surprised Banting that he would give him lab space, an assistant, and ten dogs in order to conduct his experiment. According to Banting, Dr. Macleod repeated the same phrase over and over. "It was worth trying," Banting remembered Macleod saying. "Negative results would be of great physiological value." In other words, Macleod still didn't think this mysterious Hormone X was going to cure anything. He just needed to prove he was right.

Banting wasn't terribly bothered by Macleod's lack of confidence. In reading about the work already done in tying off the pancreas, Banting learned that most of the experiments had been done by medical students with little experience in surgery. Banting's operating background would be a great benefit.

Banting wanted to get started right away. Macleod told him that was impossible. The soonest he could begin would be in the summer, when more lab space and assistants would be available. So Banting returned to London. He wasn't happy. His medical practice was still unsuccessful. His only job was part-time and low-paying. He expressed his impatience to Dr. Starr, but his mentor wrote him back that leaving the University of Western Ontario for an experiment which would probably fail was a bad idea.

One of the men who Dr. Banting trusted the most had basically told him not to waste his time experimenting with the hormone.

Although Banting wanted to do the research, he still pursued other options. He considered working as a doctor in the Indian army and unsuccessfully applied for a job as a medical officer for an oil exploration company.

People close to Banting described him as someone whose energies went in every direction. Like many young people, he was restless and having a hard time finding something he'd be good at. Edith became tired of her young fiance's instability. She broke off the engagement and returned the ring.

As far as Banting was concerned, there was no longer a good reason to stay in London. So as spring progressed, he became more and more obsessed with the idea of doing research.

The job he wanted didn't pay anything and he'd even have to cover his own expenses, but he didn't care. In his memoirs, Banting described his activities during the spring of 1921: "I read widely on the subject of carbohydrate metabolism and even read a little about diabetes. The more I read and the more I thought on the subject and the more subsidiary experiments which I planned, the more impatient I became."

Finally the day he was to leave arrived. Although he considered selling his office, Banting decided not to. In case he failed, he wanted to have someplace where he could return.

It wouldn't be necessary.

Outgoing and privileged young Charles Best had little in common with boss Frederick Banting except for two things — rural roots and a passion for research.

Chapter 6

The Best Assistant

• •

In many ways, Charles Herbert Best was the opposite of Fred Banting. The good-looking, blonde-haired, blue-eyed twenty-two-year-old was outgoing where Banting was shy. Banting's father was a farmer, Best's was a doctor. Still, they both shared rural roots as Best had grown up on the coast of Maine.

Having just graduated with his Honours Baccalaureate in Physiology and Chemistry degree from the University of Toronto, Best had a good background in laboratory techniques such as blood analysis and was already expert in blood-sugar measurement.

The next year he would be pursuing his medical studies under Dr. Macleod. He'd originally planned to take a paying job over the summer, devoting his free time to Margaret, his fiancee. Those summer plans changed when Dr. Macleod offered him the opportunity to assist Banting with his research. When Best learned what the research involved he became very interested. In 1917, diabetes had killed one of his aunts in Boston.

The position would be for half a summer, and Best flipped a coin with another man, Clark Noble, to see who would work first. Best won. The toss of a coin would change the young man's life.

When Banting met Best in mid-May of 1921, the doctor still wasn't completely sure about how they would proceed. He told Best that he would be responsible for checking the blood sugar levels of the dogs with induced diabetes. The work in hematology—

the study of blood—had changed a great deal since Banting's days as a medical student.

The pair went to the little room in the physiology department that had been assigned to them. The space was disgusting. No one had used the room for over a decade, and as Banting remembered, "it contained the dirt of the years."

Worse, the top-floor room was beneath a tar and gravel roof. It would become very hot during the notoriously unpleasant Toronto summer. When the pair went to mop the floor, water leaked to the floor below. They finally had to clean it with sponges on their hands and knees. It wasn't a very auspicious beginning for the two researchers.

Despite the challenges, Banting was excited to be in the lab. Less than a year after his post-midnight scribbling, he would finally be able to test his theory.

Banting had never done a pancreatectomy, or removal of the pancreas. It was an operation mainly done in animal research. Macleod demonstrated the operation on the first dog. The dog was anesthetized and part of the pancreas was removed. Only a remnant (which Banting called a "pedicle") was left behind. This way, the pancreas would function normally while the dog recovered from the difficult surgery. Later, this pedicle could be snipped away for a total pancreatectomy.

Without its pancreas, the dog would become diabetic. After showing the men how to do the operation, Macleod left for Scotland. He would be gone for the rest of the summer. Banting and Best were on their own.

The pair took other dogs who would have their pancreatic ducts tied off. The dogs would live fairly normally, but the pancreas would atrophy—or wither and get smaller. After a few weeks, Banting would remove it. The atrophied pancreas would still contain the living, all-important islands of Langerhans cells. Banting would then inject the material into the dogs without pancreases. Unfortunately, Banting's lack of experience with the operation led to tragic consequences.

The first few dogs they worked on died from the anesthesia or the operation itself. Every death worried Banting. Far from being a heartless researcher, Banting cared about the dogs he worked on, and didn't want to see them suffer.

Speaking about one dog who died, Banting wrote, "I have seen patients die and never shed a tear. But when that dog died, I wanted to be alone for tears would fall despite anything I could do."

At the time, animal rights groups were very powerful. In England, Dr. Banting wouldn't even have been allowed to do the research on dogs. At the University of Toronto, he was told to be careful when transporting the animals in order to avoid protests.

Banting did everything he could to keep the dogs comfortable. He kept their pens spotless, and played with them often.

He even made sure the drawing of blood was painless. While other doctors used to anesthetize dogs and cut open a vein, Banting trained them to jump up on the table so he could use a needle. By not putting them under anesthesia unnecessarily, he avoided undue risk to their lives.

Eventually, Banting learned to perform the pancreatectomies correctly. Other dogs had their pancreatic ducts tied off. After about five weeks—in early July—Banting opened up one of those dogs. The pancreas should have degenerated.

It hadn't.

Instead, the sutures he'd done had ruptured. They'd waited weeks for nothing. Banting went to the other dogs with tied-off ducts and saw a similar problem. So the next time, he sutured several times rather than just once. He often used silk thread instead of catgut, which had a tendency to loosen.

By now, the mood in the overheated lab was very tense. Banting knew he was starting to run out of time. Even worse, they were running out of dogs. Banting sold his beat-up Ford in order to buy more.

The two men continued to wait, nervous about whether or not the experiment would succeed. The pair discussed what would happen if the substance they'd discovered worked. It would change the world for diabetic patients. The two even settled on a name for the product—"isletin" after the islands of Langerhans where the product would come from.

Banting talked to his cousin Fred's wife, Lillian Hipwell, telling her that "If what I am working on is a success, I will be a famous man, but then I don't think it will happen."

Considering that Banting was broke, while his cousin and fellow medical school graduate was living a successful, stable life, it isn't surprising that Banting was racked by doubt.

On July 30, 1921, Banting took out the atrophied pancreas from a dog with its duct tied. Best sliced the pieces up and put it in a chilled laboratory mortar containing ice-cold Ringer solution, a mixture of salts in water. He ground up the half-frozen mixture, then filtered it through cheesecloth. Warmed to body temperature, what remained was pinkish colored.

At 10:15 in the morning, Banting injected it into a white terrier. The dog, its pancreas removed weeks earlier, was very diabetic. Its blood sugar at the time of the injection was very high.

The two men waited impatiently, hoping against hope. An hour later, Best carefully tested the terrier's blood sugar. The count had dropped forty percent.

The isletin worked!

"Marble desks, cushioned chairs and suites of rooms... are not the essentials of research," Banting once noted in a speech. Like many scientists of his time, Banting made life-saving breakthroughs in a lab that was cramped, dirty, and poorly equipped.

Chapter 7

Insulin!

• •

The path from the first scientific breakthrough to its successful application is seldom a clear and unbroken one. Complications almost always develop.

This was the case with isletin. Although the injection of Hormone X had lowered the blood sugar of a diabetic dog, it was barely cause for celebration. The next day the dog died.

It was then that Dr. Frederick Banting and medical student Charles Best realized the truth about what they had discovered. It wasn't a cure. It was a treatment.

Throughout the hot summer, the pair continued their experiments. Sweating in the heat of the laboratory, Banting operated on a series of dogs. Best prepared solutions made up of liver, spleen and other organs. They didn't work. Neither did those made from the whole pancreas, nor even their new solution when it was given to the dogs in any way other than by injection.

By September, Banting had two very substantial problems. The first was his usual dilemma: money. The cash from the sale of his beat-up Ford was history. He'd been working for free for months, getting extra money by performing tonsillectomies (removing tonsils) for one of his friends. He had even sold some of his instruments.

During a conversation with professor of pharmacology Velyien Henderson, Banting talked about his money problems. Sixty years later, Professor Henderson's secretary would tell the author of the book *The Story of Insulin* that Banting "put his hand in his pocket, took out seven cents and put it on the desk and said, 'There, that's all I have to live on in the world if I don't get a job.'"

Henderson believed in Banting. He knew the young doctor was performing research which someday might save lives. The professor gave Dr. Banting a part-time job as a special lecturer in pharmacology. The job paid $250 a month, equal to about three thousand dollars today.

With one problem solved, Banting had a second, more difficult dilemma. Banting and Best had discovered a method for lowering a diabetic dog's blood sugar by ligating the pancreas of another dog. Not only did the isletin take over a month to create, it basically saved the life of one dog by sacrificing another. It wasn't a technique they could use on diabetic people.

The two men's habit of carefully reading the medical literature solved their problem. Best read an article written by the French researcher G.E. Laguesse claiming that islands of Langerhans cells were more plentiful in newborns.

Excited by Best's suggestion, Banting told the idea to Professor Henderson, who didn't understand the doctor's enthusiasm. Why was it better to get islands of Langerhans cells from puppies?

Not puppies, Banting explained, but calves. He believed the material from a calf's pancreas would work in a dog. In fact, not even calves, but embryos. Banting reminded Henderson that before birth, digestive fluid isn't present. Therefore a calf embryo would be even richer in islands of Langerhans cells than a newborn's.

Henderson still didn't know where the researchers would easily obtain cow embryos. Banting's background made all the difference. He'd grown up on a farm, he told Henderson. Farmers tried to breed cows before slaughtering them because a pregnant cow will eat more and fatten up faster.

Banting believed he and Best would be able to get the raw material for their isletin at the slaughterhouse!

The next day, Best and Banting traveled to the William Davies Company's slaughterhouse in northwest Toronto. Although the owner didn't understand why the two young researchers needed calf embryos, he let them have all they wanted. The pair took them back to the medical school.

In the lab, Best carefully followed the now-familiar process. Then he handed the solution to Banting, who injected it into a diabetic dog. Once again they waited. It worked!

The two had eliminated one problem—time. No longer would they have to wait over a month for a ligated dog to produce the solution. Better still, they wouldn't have to sacrifice one dog to save another.

Despite all these advantages, it was still an imperfect solution to their problem. There would never be enough calf embryos available to treat all the human diabetics throughout the world.

Up until then, Banting's surgical experience was the main reason they'd succeeded where others had failed. Now it was Best's turn to save the day.

Best's education had been more focused on chemistry than Banting's had been. Also, in just the few years which separated them, there had been many breakthroughs. Best remembered classroom experiments where alcohol and acid were used. He tried this on an adult cow's pancreas.

The two cut up the pancreas, allowed it to stand in the alcohol-acid solution for forty-eight hours and then used a technique Macleod had shown them. They evaporated the alcohol by using a current of warm air flowing over porcelain dishes containing the solution. The dry residue was dissolved in saline solution, then injected into a diabetic dog.

They were not disappointed. The dog's blood sugar dropped by half in four hours. Although it had been Banting's original idea to get the solution by ligating a dog's pancreas, the two managed to move beyond all the problems that created.

The events of December 8th meant they were ready for the next step.

They were ready to test the treatment on people!

Banting's love for research began with the $57 microscope he purchased as a medical student.

Even eighty years ago, medical research involving animals was very controversial. Best and Banting did everything they could to keep the dogs they experimented on comfortable and happy. Still, a number of them died so that millions of diabetics might be saved.

Chapter 8

The Nobel Prize

•••

Frederick Banting and Charles Best were very close to being able to test their isletin on human subjects. Banting begged Macleod to let James Collip help them.

For weeks, whenever Banting bumped into Collip, the young biochemist said if they needed his help to let him know. Collip worked a few blocks away from the diabetes research, in the pathology building of Toronto General Hospital. Thirty years later, a fellow researcher would remember Collip telling him at the time that it would take him just two weeks to purify the isletin. It wasn't an idle boast.

Although at age twenty-nine he was just a year younger than Banting, he'd earned his Ph.D. five years earlier. Widely published, he preferred research to everything else, often working all night on experiments.

Macleod agreed to let Collip join Banting. Although his skills were needed for the work to continue, in an unpublished memoir Best recalled, "I was opposed to Collip's work for obvious and selfish reasons, but Fred Banting persuaded me not to protest too vigorously." Clark Noble, the student who'd lost the coin flip, also joined the team.

Meanwhile, Macleod put his own mark on the experiments. It wouldn't be the first time. He believed isletin's name didn't roll off the tongue, nor was it easy to spell. He insisted the new product be called "insulin." As he pointed out to Banting, the name had been suggested for Hormone X back in 1909.

Banting reluctantly agreed. The first human trial took place on January 11, 1922.

Leonard Thompson was very sick. The fourteen-year-old diabetic weighed less than 65 pounds. His parents had already prepared themselves for his death. As the young man lay dying at the Toronto General Hospital, his parents were told about a new experimental treatment. They decided to try it.

"We waited around for the first specimens and could hardly contain our suppressed excitement," Banting recalled in his memoirs. "This was in reality the first human diabetic to be treated."

But the first time insulin was tried on a human being, it failed. An abscess formed at the injection site, indicating that the insulin extract contained impurities. Thompson's sugar level barely dropped.

Despite the boy's condition, the doctors at the hospital decided to discontinue the treatment. On January 14, Macleod told a reporter with the Toronto Star, "We've really no hope to offer anyone at all as yet."

In the lab, Collip worked day and night to eliminate the extract's impurities. On January 23, Banting convinced the doctors at Toronto General to try the insulin again. At 11 a.m. it was injected into Leonard Thompson. In a paper later published by Banting and the others, the doctor wrote, "The boy became brighter, more active, looked better and said he felt stronger." The insulin was a success!

It would be impossible to overstate the impact of that day. By February, diabetics across Canada—indeed across the world—heard the news. At the

University of Toronto, Macleod dropped all of his experiments, devoting himself entirely to the task of producing and purifying the insulin.

Banting and his colleagues patented the new drug, in order to make sure that no one could market an inferior product. Unlike many researchers who become rich from their discoveries, Banting only asked for a small fee from the drug companies to cover costs.

As the drug became widely available, diabetics still journeyed to Toronto to see Dr. Banting. His fame was growing; they believed he was the best one to treat them. Despite Banting's insistence that their own doctors could administer the insulin once they were trained in its use, the diabetics continued to come to him. Eventually, Dr. Banting leased a small office on Bloor Street in Toronto.

Every morning when he arrived, he would be greeted by long lines of diabetics, some as thin and sickly as famine victims. It was an incredible change for a man who just a couple of years before had suffered through an entire month when only a single patient asked for his services.

Despite all the business, one thing remained the same: Banting refused to charge his patients even close to what other doctors were earning. When he closed the Bloor Street office, he still owed his father over four thousand dollars.

"He would give away his own breeches," the Chancellor of Toronto University once said in a speech. "You didn't have to pick his pocket; he would freely give you the contents."

His money problems finally went away in 1923. The Canadian House of Commons adopted an unprecedented resolution to pay Banting $7500 a year in recognition of his achievement. Banting became a full professor at the University of Toronto when they established the Best and Banting Chair of Medical Research. Banting had insisted that Best's name be added to the post, which had a ten thousand dollar annual budget.

The final great achievement for Banting came when he was nominated for the Nobel Prize for Medicine in 1923. Banting was unhappy when he learned that not only had Best's name been left off of the award, but also that Macleod was listed first. Macleod didn't even believe in the research when it began and went on vacation during its most crucial time. Why should he get to share the prize?

Banting considered refusing the award, but his friends talked him out of it. Instead, Banting dedicated half of his share of the forty thousand dollar award to Best. He also mentioned the man whenever he was interviewed about the discovery of insulin. Macleod, for his part, shared his money with Collip.

To this day, many consider the discovery of insulin and awarding of the Nobel Prize for Medicine to Banting and Macleod to be one of the great achievements in Canadian history.

EPILOGUE

The discovery of insulin radically transformed the lives of millions of diabetics. Among them were Dr.

George R. Minot—who discovered a treatment for the deadly disease pernicious anemia—and literary giant H.G. Wells. Both men were saved because of insulin.

The lives of its young discoverers changed as well. The life of Dr. Frederick Banting was especially altered.

Because the discovery "came out of the blue," and its chief discoverer was a little-known doctor, the attention Banting got was incredible.

In his work, Banting went from struggling with Best in a stuffy room to performing research alongside dozens of assistants in a gleaming laboratory. He explored techniques for curing cancer, and looked into insulin as a treatment for mental patients. He discovered a way to prevent the miner's illness silicosis by using metallic aluminum.

Through all of his triumphs, Banting remained the humble doctor with rural roots he'd always been. "Marble desks, cushioned chairs and suites of rooms in buildings of fine architecture are not the essentials of research...Pasteur and Barnard worked in a cellar," he said in a speech before a medical organization.

Banting's personal life changed as well. On June 4, 1925, he married Marion Robertson, a radiology technician at Toronto General Hospital. Although they divorced in 1932, the marriage bore Banting his only child. William Robertson Banting was born in 1929.

As part of his research, Banting traveled widely. He braved harsh Arctic weather in order to report on the health conditions of Eskimos. He visited Russia, a country where the doctor was so well known that he was recognized on the street and treated like a celebrity. He also had a chance to meet with England's King

George V shortly after the insulin discovery.

Over ten years later, England acknowledged the scientist's contribution by naming him Knight Commander of the Civil Division of the Order of the British Empire. Dr. Banting was now Sir Banting.

A smiling Banting accompanies his new bride, radiology technician Marion Robertson

In 1939, he remarried, this time to Henrietta Ball, who did work in cancer research.

Across the Atlantic, war was once again ravaging Europe. Banting had been strongly opposed to Adolph Hitler's quest for power; in his work the doctor met regularly with Jewish researchers who'd fled the Nazis in Europe.

So not long after his second marriage, Banting rejoined the Army. Although he pleaded for the chance to work with a combat unit overseas, the Canadian government refused Banting's request. They believed he was too important to be risked.

Instead of going overseas, Banting was put in charge of a large-scale research program. He worked to overcome the dangers faced by pilots when they flew at high altitudes. Often these men would black out or suffer the bends—air bubbles forming in the blood. These problems often had deadly consequences.

Banting developed a special flight suit, which was filled with fluid intended to protect the lives of airmen when they flew at great heights. In February of 1941, Banting's colleague in the project traveled by ship across the Atlantic to England with the suits. Banting chose to fly.

Shortly after the plane took off from Canada and began to cross over the Atlantic, its engines failed. The pilot managed to turn back. He crash-landed in a deserted part of Newfoundland, tearing off a wing and damaging the plane. Banting was severely injured and two other men were killed. Without radio contact, the pilot and the plane were stranded for two days.

While waiting for rescue, Banting died on February 21.

At his birthplace in Alliston, a plaque has been erected in his honor. It reads, in part, "From his parents he learned inquisitiveness, resourcefulness, persistence, sincerity, and true godliness. Always fond of dogs during his boyhood, Dr. Banting was later to experiment with these animals in the discovery of insulin. Life and hope resulted for diabetics worldwide."

Eighty years later, Dr. Banting's discovery remains the primary treatment for diabetes. There is still no cure.

Frederick Banting Chronology

- 1891, is born in Alliston, Ontario, in Canada.
- 1910, registers at Victoria College in Toronto, Canada majoring in theology.
- 1912, enrolls in medicine at the University of Toronto.
- 1916, graduates from medical school; serves in World War I.
- 1918, wounded at 2nd Battle of Cambrai, France; receives Military Cross for courage under fire.
- 1919, begins working at Hospital for Sick Children, in Toronto, Canada.
- 1920, opens private practice in London, Ontario.
- 1920, convinces Dr. J.J.R. Macleod to support his research at University of Toronto.
- 1921, working with Charles Best, discovers that pancreas extract injected into a dog lowers its blood sugar.
- 1922, test on human proves insulin lowers blood sugar in diabetes.
- 1923, shares Nobel Prize for Medicine with Macleod; asks that Best's contribution also be acknowledged.
- 1925, marries Marion Robertson.
- 1929, has a son, William Robertson Banting.
- 1932, divorces Marion Robertson.
- 1934, knighted by Britain.
- 1939, marries Henrietta Ball; rejoins Army.
- 1941, is killed after a plane crash in Newfoundland while on wartime medical mission.

Insulin Timeline

- **2000 B.C.**: Egyptian hieroglyphics describe diabetes.
- **100 A.D.**: Greek physician Arataeus gives name "diabetes" to disease.
- **early 1800s**: chemical tests developed to indicate and measure presence of sugar in urine.
- **1869**: German medical student Paul Langerhans discovers second set of cells in pancreas.
- **1870**: French doctor A. Bouchardt develops exercise and diet regimes to treat diabetics.
- **1889**: German scientists Oskar Minkowski and Joseph von Mering discover that removal of pancreas in a dog causes it to become diabetic. Also learned that tying (ligating) pancreatic ducts did not cause diabetes.
- **1901**: American doctor Eugene Opie showed diabetes was caused by damaging "islands of Langerhans" cells.
- **1902**: E.H. Starling coins the term "hormone" to describe chemical messengers such as the "islands of Langerhans" cells.
- **1919**: Frederick Allen's book, "Total Dieting Regulation in the Treatment of Diabetes" is published, and his radical method saves many lives.
- **1922**: Frederick Banting, working with Charles Best, discovers insulin, a new treatment for diabetes.

For Further Reading

Books for children and young adults:

Levine, I.E. *The Discoverer of Insulin: Dr. Frederick G. Banting,* Julian Messner, Inc., New York, 1959.

Mayer, Ann Margaret. *Sir Frederick Banting, Doctor Against Diabetes,* Mankato, Minn.: Chicago: Creative Education; distributed by Children's Press, 1974.

McCarthy, Tom. *Frederick Banting and Charles Best, Discovers of Insulin,* Illustrated by Krista Johnson. Ottawa: Novalis, 1982.

Rowland, John. *The Insulin Man: The Story of Sir Frederick Banting,* New York: Roy Publishers, 1966, c.1965.

Webb, Michael, ed. *Frederick Banting: Discoverer of Insulin,* Missauga, Ontario: Copp Clark Pittman, 1991.

On the Web:

The Discovery of Insulin (National Film Board) http://www.onf.ca/FMT/E/MSN/14/14421.html

The Discovery of Insulin: Banting, Best, Collip, Macleod. On-Line History Resource Centre. http://www.discoveryofinsulin.com

The Quest (National Film Board). http://www.onf.ca/FMT/E/MSN/11/11774.html

Sir Frederick Grant Banting. http://almaz.com/nobel/medicine/1923a.html

Visit the Banting Museum and Education Centre. http://www.diabetes.ca/banting/banting.html

Heritage Project. http://www.heritageproject.ca/media/minutes/expanded/ssflem.html

Glossary of Terms

amputate - cut off or remove a limb, usually in surgery.

anesthesia/anesthetic - a substance, either gases or drugs that are injected, used to cause the loss of physical sensation that permits patients to be operated on without pain.

Bunsen burner - a metal tube in a laboratory connected to a gas source; small laboratory burner.

cell - tiniest unit of organism capable of independent life.

diabetes - a disease in which a person loses the ability to utilize food.

duct - a tube within the body through which material flows.

insulin - a hormone in the pancreas which prevents diabetes.

ligate - to tie or bind.

microscope - instrument used to magnify objects too small to be seen with the naked eye.

orthopedics - area of medicine dealing with the repair of injuries or deformities in the skeletal structure (bones).

pancreas - a long, irregular shaped gland lying behind the stomach.

pancreatectomy- removal of the pancreas.

Index